Happiness Over Everything

CHOOSE YOURSELF ALWAYS

Discover The Hidden Wonders of Looking Within and Finding Peace

HANNAH WARD

Table of Contents

Chapter 1: Happy People Have A Morning Ritual 6
Chapter 2: If Today Was Your Last Day 8
Chapter 3: Happy People Are Optimistic 11
Chapter 4: *How to Stop Chasing New Goals All the Time* 14
Chapter 5: Things That Steal Your Motivation 17
Chapter 6: Happy People Spend Time Alone 20
Chapter 7: Your Work is Good Enough 23
Chapter 8: Happy People Do What Matters to Them 26
Chapter 9: How Much Is Your Time Really Worth? 28
Chapter 10: *Happy People Give Freely* 30
Chapter 11: Why Are You Working So Hard 33
Chapter 12: 8 Ways To Deal With Setbacks In Life 37
Chapter 13: 8 Ways To Gain Self-Confidence 43
Chapter 14: *What To Do When You Feel Like Your Work is not Good Enough* 47
Chapter 15: 8 Ways To Love Yourself First 50
Chapter 16: *7 Ways On How To Attract Success In Life* 54
Chapter 17: Happy People View Problems as Challenges 58
Chapter 18: How To Take Action 61
Chapter 19: Creating Successful Habits 66
Chapter 20: Overcoming the Fear of Failure 71
Chapter 21: Why You Are Amazing 74
Chapter 22: Discovering Your Purpose 77
Chapter 23: Happy People Don't Hold on To Grudges 80
Chapter 24: Showing Up 82
Chapter 25: Enjoying The Simple Things 85
Chapter 26: 10 Reasons Money Can't Buy You Happiness 87
Chapter 27: 6 Steps To Focus On Growth 93

Chapter 28: *Be Motivated by Challenge* 98

Chapter 29: Consistency can bring you happiness. 101

Chapter 30: Enjoying The Journey 106

Chapter 31: "Happy People Enjoy the Hidden Pleasures life has to offer." 109

Chapter 32: Happy People Focus on What They Are Good at 111

Chapter 33: Why Spending Time with Friends Can Buy You Happiness 113

Chapter 34: How Will You Choose To Live Your Life? 115

Chapter 1:
Happy People Have A Morning Ritual

For many of us, mornings begin in a rushed panic. We allow our alarm clocks to buzz at least a dozen times before deciding we have to get out of bed. Then we rush around our homes half-awake, trying to get ready for our day. In a hurry, we stub our toe on the bedpost, forget to put on deodorant, and don't pack a lunch because we simply don't have time. It's no wonder that so many folks despise the thought of being awake before 9 a.m.!

So it may not surprise you to know that the happiest and healthiest people tend to enjoy their mornings. They appear to thrive on waking up with the sun and look forward to a new day of possibilities. These people have humble morning rituals that increase their sense of well-being and give their day purpose.

Here are 3 morning habits that healthy and happy people tend to share:

1. **They wake up with a sense of gratitude**

Practicing gratitude is associated with a sense of overall happiness and a better mood—so it makes sense that the happiest and healthiest people we know start the day with a gratitude practice. This means that they're truly appreciative of their life and all of its little treasures. They practice small acts of gratitude in the morning by expressing thankfulness to their partner each morning before they rise from bed. They may also write about their gratefulness for five minutes each morning in a journal that they keep by their bedside.

2. They begin every morning anew.

The happiest and healthiest people know that every day is a brand-new day—a chance to start over and do something different. Yesterday may have been a complete failure for them, but today is a new day for success and adventure. Individuals who aren't ruined by one bad day are resilient creatures. <u>Resiliency</u> is a telltale sign of having purpose and happiness.

3. They take part in affirmation, meditation, or prayer.

Many of the happiest folks alive are <u>spiritual</u>. Affirmations are a way of reminding ourselves of all that we have going for us, and they allow us to engrain in our minds the kind of person we wish to be. <u>Meditation</u> helps keep our mind focused, calms our nerves, and supports inner peace. If you're already spiritual, prayer is a great way to connect and give thanks for whatever higher power you believe in.

Chapter 2:
If Today Was Your Last Day

If today was your last day, what would you do with your life? Steve Jobs once said that "For the past 33 years, I have looked in trhe mirror every morning and asked myself: '**If today** were the **last day** of my life, would I want to do what I am about to do **today**? ' And whenever the answer has been 'No' for too many **days** in a row, I know I need to change something.".

Do you agree with that statement? For me I believe that it is true to a certain extent. I argue that not many of us have the luxury of doing what we love to do every single day. As much as we want to work at that dream job or earn that great salary, or whatever that ideal may be, for some of us who have to feed a family or make ends meet, it is just not possible. And we choose to make that sacrifice to work at a job that we may not like, or go through a routine that sometimes might seem a drag. But that's a personal choice that we choose to make and that is okay too.

On the flip side, i do believe that for those who have the luxury and the choice to pursue whatever careers, dreams, hobbies, and interests we want to pursue, that we should go for it and not live life in regret. I have heard of countless friends who work at a job they hate day in and day out, complaining about their life every single day and about how miserable they are, but are too afraid to leave that job in fear of not being able to find something they like or in fear that their dreams would not work out. Not because they couldn't afford to do so, but because they are afraid. This fear keeps them trapped in a never ending cycle of unhappiness and missed opportunities.

Personally, I'm in the camp of doing something you dislike even if u struggle with it if it can provide you with some financial security and pay your bills, whilst at the same time pursuing your dreams part time just to test the waters. You have the comfort of a monthly stream of income while also taking a leap of faith and going after what you really want to do in life. And who knows it could work out some day. In the present moment, I'm actually working on many different interests and hobbies. I do the necessary work that i hate but explore other areas that brings me joy, and that is what keeps be going. I have a passion for singing, songwriting, tennis, and making videos like this that not only educates but also aims to bring joy to others. My full-time job only fulfils my bank account while my interests and work that i do on the side fulfils my heart and soul. And who knows, if any one of these side hobbies turn out into something that I can make some money with, hey it's a win win situation now don't you think?

I challenge each and every one of you to go ahead and take a leap of faith. Time waits for no one and you never know when your last day might be. Koby Bryant died suddenly from a helicopter crash at a young age of 41. But I would argue that because he pursued his dreams at a young age, he has already lived a wonderful and fulfilling life as opposed to someone who is too afraid to do what they want and hasn't lived up to their fullest potential despite living until 90. You have also heard of Chadwick Boseman who was immortalised as a great human being who gave it his all despite fighting colon cancer. He pursued his dreams and I bet that he had no regrets that his life had to end earlier than it should. And to Steve jobs, he gave us Apple, the biggest company in the world by pursuing his dream of changing the world and the way we communicate with one another. Without him we wouldn't have all our favourite beloved apple products that we use today. Without him there might not be amazon, google, Facebook because there wouldn't be apps and there wouldn't be devices that people used to do all these things with.

But most importantly, this is about you. How do you want to live your life, and if today was your last day, what would you do differently and how would this carry on to all other areas of your life. Your relationships with your family, your relationship with your friends, your partner. And do you feel fulfilled as a human being or do you feel empty inside. It is never too late to turn your life around and make choices that will make your heart fill with immense joy and gratitude until your life truly ends. So make the decision right now to honour yourself by living your day to the fullest, coz you never know when it might be your last.

Chapter 3:
Happy People Are Optimistic

Beyond the simple reality that optimists are happier people (and happiness is what you're striving for), optimism has other benefits as well. So, if you want to achieve greater happiness, try being optimistic for a day.

Optimists enjoy a greater degree of academic success than pessimists do. Because optimistic students think it's possible for them to make a good grade, they study hardier and they study smarter. They manage the setting in which they study and they seek help from others when they need it. (Optimism, it turns out, is almost as predictive of how well students do in college as the SAT.)

Optimists are more self-confident than pessimists are. They believe in *themselves* more than fate.

Optimists are more likely to be problem-solvers than pessimists are. When pessimistic students get a D on a test, they tend to think things like: "I knew I shouldn't have taken this course. I'm no good at psychology." The optimistic student who gets a D says to herself, "I can do better. I just didn't study enough for this test. I'll do better next time." And she will.

Optimists welcome second chances after they fail more than pessimists do. Optimistic golfers always take a *mulligan* (a redo swing without penalty). Why? Because they expect to achieve a better result the second time around.

Optimists are more socially outgoing than pessimists are. Socially outgoing folks believe that the time they spend with other human beings makes them better in some way — smarter, more interesting, more attractive. Unfortunately, pessimists see little, if any, benefit from venturing out into the social world.

Optimists are not as lonely as pessimists are. Because pessimists don't see as much benefit from socializing with others, they have far fewer social and emotional connections in their lives, which is what loneliness is all about.

Optimists utilize social support more effectively than pessimists do. They aren't afraid to reach out in times of need.

Optimists are less likely to blame others for their misfortune than pessimists are. When you blame someone else for your troubles, what you're really saying is, "You're the *cause* of my problem and, therefore, you have to be the *solution* as well." Optimists have just as many troubles as pessimists throughout life — they just accept more responsibility for dealing with their misfortune.

Optimists cope with stress better than pessimists do. Pessimists worry, optimists act. A patient with coronary heart disease who is pessimistic "hopes and prays" that he doesn't have another heart attack anytime soon. The optimistic heart patient leaves little to chance — instead, he exercises regularly, practices his meditation exercises, adheres to a low-cholesterol diet, and makes sure he always gets a good night's sleep.

Chapter 4:
How to Stop Chasing New Goals All the Time

The philosopher Alan Watts always said that life is like a song, and the sole purpose of the song is to dance. He said that when we listen to a song, we don't dance to get to the end of the music. We dance to enjoy it. This isn't always how we live our lives. Instead, we rush through our moments, thinking there's always something better, there's always some goal we need to achieve.

"Existence is meant to be fun. It doesn't go anywhere; it just is." Our lives are not about things and status. Even though we've made ourselves miserable with wanting, we already have everything we need. Life is meant to be lived. If you can't quit your job tomorrow, enjoy where you are. Focus on the best parts of every day. Believe that everything you do has a purpose and a place in the world.

Happiness comes from <u>gratitude</u>. You're alive, you have people to miss when you go to work, and you get to see them smile every day. We all have to do things we don't want to do; we have to survive. When you find yourself working for things that don't matter, like a big house or a fancy car, when you could be living, you've missed the point. You're playing the song, but you're not dancing.

"A song isn't just the ending. It's not just the goal of finishing the song. The song is an experience."

We all think that everything should be amazing when we're at the top, but it's not. Your children have grown older, and you don't remember the little things.

"...tomorrow and plans for tomorrow can have no significance at all unless you are in full contact with the reality of the present since it is in the present and only in the present that you live."

You feel cheated of your time, cheated by time. Now you have to make up for it. You have to live, make the most of what you have left. So you set another goal.

This time you'll build memories and see places, do things you never got the chance to do. The list grows, and you wonder how you'll get it all done and still make your large mortgage payment. You work more hours so you can do all this stuff "someday." You've overwhelmed yourself again.

You're missing the point.

Stop wanting more, <u>be grateful for</u> today. Live in the moment. Cherish your life and the time you have in this world. If it happens, it happens. If it doesn't, then it wasn't meant to; let it go.

"We think if we don't interfere, it won't happen."

There's always an expectation, always something that has to get done. You pushed aside living so that you could live up to an expectation that doesn't exist to anyone but you. The expectation is always there because you gave it power. To live, you've got to let it go.

You save all your money so that you can retire. You live to retire. Then you get old, and you're too tired to live up to the expectation you had of retirement; you never realize your dreams.

At forty, you felt cheated; at eighty, you are cheated. You cheated yourself the whole way through to the end.

"Your purpose was to dance until the end, but you were so focused on the end that you forgot to dance."

Chapter 5:
Things That Steal Your Motivation

Motivation seems a common word, sometimes a bit overrated. But it matters to those who haven't had one good moment for a long time.

The person who has everything might not like to talk about motivation. But the person who struggles and after some time gives up needs some motivation to keep going and keep doing so that he has something to achieve and live for.

Motivation is central to a good and productive life but most people lose it too soon. Some know how to regain it but some don't have a single clue what got them distracted.

Fear is a generic flaw in every human's life. People tend to fear the simplest of things and the simplest of feelings. Some call it a phobia, some call it hesitation or someone might call it smart planning.

The fact is that you don't have what it takes to do what you are reluctant to do. It may be due to fear of failure or fear of getting laughed at.

Fear keeps you from trying things that are easy to excel at and require absolutely no effort rather determination, and taking away one's determination is the direct path to demotivation

You fear something so you avoid taking a step and hence you lack the hard work that is elementary to everything in life.

Not working to your full potential is another thing that keeps the best outcomes at bay. The outcomes might surprise you and might motivate you to work even harder for the diamonds that lie ahead.

The thing that made us evolve as a human and has lead to all things we have achieved till now is competition. The competition requires us to compare our present to someone better than us and this comparison doesn't always work well for us.

We have to accept the fact that there are people more deserving and more achieved than us. But these feelings shouldn't keep us lying around and not doing to get to that place too. We have everything in life if we have a healthy body and air in our lungs. What you need more is a little motivation to get closer to the ones you idealize.

This Inferiority complex makes us wait for something to happen on its own. But what you should be doing is to get up, tie those shoes and run towards what you want. You cannot expect something to be served to you with you sitting there all day.

Chances don't come in a lottery. Fortune favors those who take risks and want to create chances. Even if you miss one chance, don't take it hard on yourself. You don't need to condemn yourself for one lost chance unless you have the same attitude when the next chance comes knocking around.

Motivation isn't a lost cause till you haven't knocked on all doors. When you have no doubts remaining, you will be successful on every next step.

Chapter 6:
Happy People Spend Time Alone

No man is an island except for similarly as we blossom with human contact and connections, so too would we be able to prosper from time burned through alone. Also, this, maybe, turns out to be particularly important right now since we're all in detachment. We've since quite a while ago slandered the individuals who decide to be distant from everyone else, except isolation shouldn't be mistaken for forlornness. Here are two mental reasons why investing energy in isolation makes us more joyful and more satisfied:

1. Spending time alone reconnects us.

Our inclination for isolation might be transformative, as indicated by an examination distributed in the British Journal of Psychology in 2016. Utilizing what they call "the Savannah hypothesis of satisfaction," transformative clinicians Satoshi Kanazawa of the London School of Economics and Norman Li of Singapore Management University accept that the single, tracker accumulate way of life of our precursors structure the establishment of what satisfies us in present-day times. The group examined a study of 15,000 individuals matured somewhere between 18 and 28 in the United States. They found that individuals living in more thickly populated regions were fundamentally less cheerful than the individuals who lived in more modest networks.

"The higher the populace thickness of the prompt climate, the less glad" respondents were. The scientists accept this is because we had advanced mentally from when mankind, for the most part, existed on distant, open savannahs. Since quite a while ago, we have instilled an inclination to be content alone, albeit current life generally neutralizes that. Also, as good to beat all, they tracked down that the more clever an individual was, the more they appreciated investing energy alone. Along these lines, isolation makes you more joyful AND is evidence of your smarts. We're in.

2. Spending Time Alone Teaches Us Empathy

Investing in a specific measure of energy alone can create more compassion towards others than a milestone concentrate from Harvard. Scientists found that when enormous gatherings of individuals encircle us, it's harder for us to acquire viewpoints and tune into the sensations of others. However, when we venture outside that unique circumstance, the extra headspace implies we can feel for the situation of individuals around us in a more genuine and significant manner. Furthermore, that is uplifting news for others, but different investigations show that compassion and helping other people are significant to prosperity and individual satisfaction.

"At the point when you invest energy with a specific friend network or your colleagues, you foster a 'we versus them' attitude," clarifies psychotherapist and creator Amy Morin. "Investing energy alone assists you with growing more empathy for individuals who may not find a way into your 'inward circle.' "On the off chance that you're not used to isolation, it can feel awkward from the outset," she adds. "However, making that tranquil time for yourself could be critical to turning into the best form of yourself."

Chapter 7:
Your Work is Good Enough

We, humans, are genetically coded to get mad at people getting better at things than us, if not jealous.

These feelings may not bother us right now, and they might never. But these feelings are a leech on their own. They need one to feel low on their self-esteem and may never get ahead of our selves.

We get caught in a competition that no one else imposed on us but we ourselves decided to step into it.

So what we want is one thing, but what we have and we don't want is a whole new problem. We look at one thing and want it instantly without even weighing it side by side with what we already have.

What you have right now is something you have worked for till now. It is something your fate has chosen for you. This is what might be the best for you. You don't necessarily need something better that you like over what you already have. You just need to come to terms with what you have right now and perfect your craft.

You want something more because you are not content with everything you have and everything you do. It is natural to feel this way. It is normal to want more. But it is never OK to leave a thing incomplete and just because you haven't got a hold of things yet.

Things often seem wrong. We feel like an Impostor every time we come up with something new.

Everything we do seem to be a derivative of something someone else has done because we rarely come across a unique idea these days. And even when we come across one, someone else gets the same epiphany. So we never get ahead of ourselves and compete with what is on our hands.

You already have a lot in your hands to take care of so you don't need to pet more worries. You don't need to feed your brain more weaknesses of yourself than you already have.

We all need to realize a simple fact. The fact is that no matter how much we try to second guess our achievements or failures for that matter, we will always finally come to realize that we were right the first time.

You were RIGHT the FIRST TIME. So you only needed to overcome the fight within you.

The first time we do something good, we instantly know that we have something good going on. But then we try to see through others' eyes and lose our own sight of the bigger goals.

So your work is never based on your luck, but only on your talent and devotion. And if no one steps up to give you a round of applause, you still have your own will and mind to be the best judge and critic of your deed. But you also need to become the biggest mentor and coach of your own vessel. Because no vessel without a knock shows its presence.

Chapter 8:
Happy People Do What Matters to Them

Think about what you want most out of life. What were you created for? What is your mission in life? What is your passion? You were put on this earth for a reason, and knowing that reason will help you determine your priorities.

I spent a total of four months in the hospital, healing from my sickness. During that time, I spent a lot of time thinking about my purpose in life. I discovered that my purpose is to help you change your lives by focusing on what matters most to you.

1. **Create A Plan**

Create a plan to get from where you are today to where you want to be. Maybe you need a new job. Maybe you need to go back to school. Maybe you need to deal with some relationship issues. Whatever it is, create a plan that will get you to where you want to be.

While I was in the hospital, I began to draft my life plan. My plan guides all of my actions, helps me focus on my relationships with my wife and daughter, and helps me keep working toward my life purpose. A life plan will help you focus your life too.

2. **Focus On Now**

Stop multitasking and focus on one thing at a time. It may be a project at work. It may be a conversation with your best friend. It may just be the book that you have wanted to read for months. The key is to focus on one thing at a time.

I plan each day the night before by picking the three most important tasks from my to-do list. In the morning, I focus on each one of these tasks individually until they are completed. Once I complete these three tasks, I check email, return phone calls, etc.

3. Just Say "No."

We all have too much to do and too little time. The only way you will find the time for the things that matter is to say "no" to the things that don't.

I use my purpose and life plan to make decisions about the projects and tasks I say yes to. If a project or task is not aligned with my purpose, a good fit with my life plan, and sometimes that I have time to accomplish, I say no to the project. Saying no to good opportunities gives you time to focus on the best opportunities.

Research tells us that 97 percent of people are living their life by default and not by design. They don't know where their life is headed and don't plan what they want to accomplish in life.

These steps will help you to decide what matters most to you. They will help you to begin living your life by design and not by default. Most importantly, they will help you to create a life focused on what matters to you.

Let me end by asking, "What matters most to you?

Chapter 9:
How Much Is Your Time Really Worth?

What is the biggest mistake we make in life? Perhaps Buddha's most suitable answer was given by "The biggest mistake is you think you have time." While our time in this world is free, it's also priceless. We can neither own it nor keep it, but we can use it and spend it. And once it's all lost, it's inevitable that we will never get it back.

"Your time is limited, so don't waste it living someone else's life." - Steve Jobs. Our time is limited in this world is both good and bad news. The bad news is that time flies and never returns, but the good news is that we're the pilot. The average person lives 78 years on this planet. We spend almost one-third of our lives sleeping; that's approximately 28.3 years from our lives. And still, 30% of us struggle to sleep well. We spend almost 10.5 years of our life working, but over 50% of us want to leave our current jobs. Time is a valuable asset, even more so than money. We can get more money, but we can never get more time.

After all of the years we spend doing chores, shopping, grooming, eating, drinking, TV, and social media, time leaves us with only nine years. Now the question arises, how will we spend that time? Just like we would never waste our money on something gratuitous, why do we waste our time on it? We might think that people are wasting our time when we are the ones permitting them to do that in reality. We sometimes end up losing our most beloved people because we don't value their time. Some of us don't recognize their importance until they're gone.

Every day, from the moment we wake up till the moment we get back to sleep, two voices are battling inside our heads; one wants to uplift us and one that holds us back. And which one will win? The one that we listen to the most. The one that we feed us the most. The one that we amplify. Similarly, it's up to us and our choice how we use that time in our hands. William Shakespeare once said, "Time is prolonged for those who want, very fast for those who are scared, very long for those who are sad, and very short for those who celebrate, but for those who love, time is eternal." We should make the most out of our time and learn its value by carefully analyzing what life teaches us about it.

Chapter 10:
Happy People Give Freely

"For it is in giving that we receive." - Saint Francis of Assisi.

A Chinese saying goes by, "If you want happiness for an hour, take a nap. If you want happiness for a day, go fishing. If you want happiness for a year, inherit a fortune. If you want happiness for a lifetime, help somebody." It is indeed better to give than to receive. Scientific research provides compelling anecdotal evidence that giving is a powerful pathway to personal growth and lasting happiness. When we give freely, our brain stimulates endorphins and blesses us with a feeling of euphoria. Altruism is hardwired in our brains and tends to provide us with pleasure. Helping others is a secret to living a happier and healthier, wealthier, productive, and more meaningful life.

Whether it's a charity, a piece of advice, a helping hand of any sort, or supporting someone throughout their journey, researchers Dunn, Aknin, Akin, and Norton performed a study. They showed that there is, in fact, a link between generosity and happier life. The gesture of caring about other people and doing something to improve their quality of life is the source of happiness. Once you start giving, you will feel more content and happier, and there will be no going back. You will get addicted to helping others and to the feeling that follows.

A group of psychologists from the University of California Santa Barbara conducted a study to ascertain if generosity is part of human nature. The observation showed that being a giver is more fulfilling than being a receiver and that generosity is deeply embedded in our systems. "You don't need to become a self-sacrificing martyr to feel happier. Just being a little more generous will suffice," says Prof. Tobler.

High-generosity respondents appeared not only happier but happier more often. This overarching sense of happiness in high-generosity individuals may positively affect their higher likelihood of finding life more meaningful. They were also 20% more likely to be optimistic about their future, be proud of themselves, and find enjoyment in their jobs. It's no secret that you have to give a little to get a little. The more generous you are too loved ones, acquaintances, or even strangers, the more likely those selfless deeds will be reciprocated sometime down the line. Neuroeconomics found in a recent study that merely promising to be more generous is enough to trigger a change in our brain that will eventually make us happier.

In a 2006 study, Jorge Moll and colleagues at the National Institutes of Health found that when people give, it could be anything; it activates the warm glow effect, regions of the brain associated with pleasure, social connection, and trust. Whatever you are giving to people, society, or nature, you will find yourself benefiting from a hefty dose of happiness in the process. When you express your gratitude in words or actions, you not only boost your positivity but other people's as well. The more we give, the more we stand to gain purpose, meaning, and happiness – all of the things we look for in life but are so hard to find.

Chapter 11:
Why Are You Working So Hard

Your why,
your reason to get up in the morning,
the reason you act,
really is everything - for without it, there could be nothing.
Your why is the partner of your what,
that is what you want to achieve, your ultimate goal.
Your why will be what pushes you through the hard times on the path to your dreams.

It may be your children or a burning desire to help those less fortunate,
whatever the reason may be,
it is important to keep that in mind when faced with troubles or distractions.

Knowing what you want to do, and why you are doing it,
is of imperative importance for your life.
The tragedy is that most people are aiming for nothing.
They couldn't tell you why they are working in a certain field even if they tried.
Apart from the obvious financial payment,
They have no clue why they are there.

Is financial survival alone really a good motive to act?
Or would financial prosperity be guaranteed if you pursued greater personal preference?
Whatever your ambitions or preference in life,
make sure your why is important enough to you to guarantee your persistence.

Sometimes when pursuing a burning desire,
we can become distracted from the reason we are working.

Your why should be reflected in everything you do.
Once you convince yourself that your reason is important enough, you will not stop.
Despite the hardships, despite the fear, despite the loss and pain.
As long as you maintain a steady path of faith and resilience,
your work will soon start to pay off.
A light will protrude from the darkness and the illusionary troubles sent to test your faith will disappear as if they were never here.

Your why must be strong.
Your what must be as clear as the day is to you now.
And your faith must be eternal and unwavering.
Only then will the doors be opened to you.
This dream can be real, and will be.

When it is clear in the mind with faith, the world will move to show you the way.

The way will be revealed piece by piece, requiring you to take action and do the required work to bring your dream into reality.

Your why is so incredibly important.
The bigger your why, the greater the urgency, and the quicker your action will be.

Take the leap of faith.
Do what you didn't even know you could.
Never mind anyone else.
Taking the unknown path.
Perhaps against the advice of your family and friend,
But you know what your heart wants.

You know that even though the path will be dangerous, the reward will be tremendous.
The risks of not never finding out is too great.
The risk of never knowing if you could have done better is unfathomable.
You can always do better, and you must.

Knowing what is best for you may prove to be the most important thing for you.
How you feel about the work you are doing,
How you feel about the life you are living,
And how do you make the most of the time you have on this earth.
These may prove far more important than financial reward could ever do for you.

Aim to strike a balance.

A balance between working on what you are passionate about and building a wealthy financial life.

If your why and will are strong enough,

Success is all but guaranteed for you – no second guesses needed.

Aim for the sky,

However high you make it,

you will have proven you can indeed fly.

Chapter 12:
8 Ways To Deal With Setbacks In Life

Life is never the same for anyone - It is an ever-changing phenomenon, making you go through all sorts of highs and lows. And as good times are an intrinsic part of your life, so are bad times. One day you might find yourself indebted by 3-digit figures while having only $40 in your savings account. Next day, you might be vacationing in Hawaii because you got a job that you like and pays $100,000 a year. There's absolutely no certainty to life (except passing away) and that's the beauty of it. You never know what is in store for you. But you have to keep living to see it for yourself. Setbacks in life cannot be avoided by anyone. Life will give you hardships, troubles, break ups, diabetes, unpaid bills, stuck toilet and so much more. It's all a part of your life.

Here's 8 ways that you might want to take notes of, for whenever you may find yourself in a difficult position in dealing with setback in life.

1. **Accept and if possible, embrace it**

The difference between accepting and embracing is that when you accept something, you only believe it to be, whether you agree or disagree. But when you embrace something, you truly KNOW it to be true and accept it as a whole. There is no dilemma or disagreement after you have embraced something.

So, when you find yourself in a difficult situation in life, accept it for what it is and make yourself whole-heartedly believe that this problem in your life, at this specific time, is a part of your life. This problem is what makes you complete. This problem is meant for you and only you can go through it. And you will. Period. There can be no other way.

The sooner you embrace your problem, the sooner you can fix it. Trying to bypass it will only add upon your headaches.

2. Learn from it

Seriously, I can't emphasize how important it is to LEARN from the setbacks you face in your life. Every hardship is a learning opportunity. The more you face challenges, the more you grow. Your capabilities expand with every issue you solve—every difficulty you go through, you rediscover yourself. And when you finally deal off with it, you are reborn. You are a new person with more wisdom and experience.

When you fail at something, try to explore why you failed. Be open-minded about scrutinizing yourself. Why couldn't you overcome a certain situation? Why do you think of this scenario as a 'setback'? The moment you find the answers to these questions is the moment you will have found the solution.

3. **Execute What You Have Learnt**

The only next step from here is to execute that solution and make sure that the next time you face a similar situation, you'll deal with it by having both your arms tied back and blindfolded. All you have to do is remember what you did in a similar past experience and reapply your previous solution.

Thomas A. Edison, the inventor of the light bulb, failed 10,000 times before finally making it. And he said "I have not failed. I just found 10,000 ways that won't work".

The lesson here is that you have to take every setback as a lesson, that's it.

4. **Without shadow, you can never appreciate light**

This metaphor is applicable to all things opposite in this universe. Everything has a reciprocal; without one, the other cannot exist. Just as without shadow, we wouldn't have known what light is, similarly, without light, we could've never known about shadow. The two opposites identify and complete each other.

Too much of philosophy class, but to sum it up, your problems in life, ironically, is exactly why you can enjoy your life. For example, if you are a chess player, then defeating other chess players will give you enjoyment while getting defeated will give you distress. But, when you are a chess prodigy—you have defeated every single chess player on earth and there's no one else to defeat, then what will you do to derive pleasure? Truth is, you can now no longer enjoy chess. You have no one to defeat. No one gives you the fear of losing anymore and as a result, the taste of winning has lost its appeal to you.

So, whenever you face a problem in life, appreciate it because without it, you can't enjoy the state of not having a problem. Problems give you the pleasure of learning from them and solving them.

5. View Every Obstacle As an opportunity

This one's especially for long term hindrances to your regular life. The COVID-19 pandemic for instance, has set us back for almost two years now. As distressing it is, there is also some positive impact of it. A long-term setback opens up a plethora of new avenues for you to explore. You suddenly get a large amount of time to experiment with things that you have never tried before.

When you have to pause a regular part of your life, you can do other things in the meantime. I believe that every one of us has a specific talent and most people never know what their talent is simply because they have never tried that thing.

6. Don't Be Afraid to experiment

People pursue their whole life for a job that they don't like and most of them never ever get good at it. As a result, their true talent gets buried under their own efforts. Life just carries on with unfound potential. But when some obstacle comes up and frees you from the clutches of doing what you have been doing for a long time, then you should get around and experiment. Who knows? You, a bored high school teacher, might be a natural at tennis. You won't know it unless you are fired from that job and actually play tennis to get over it. So whenever life gives you lemons, quit trying to hold on to it. Move on and try new things instead.

7. Stop Comparing yourself to others

The thing is, we humans are emotional beings. We become emotionally vulnerable when we are going through something that isn't supposed to be. And in such times, when we see other people doing fantastic things in life, it naturally makes us succumb to more self-loathing. We think lowly of our own selves and it is perfectly normal to feel this way. Talking and comapring ourselves to people who are seemingly untouched by setbacks is a counterproductive move. You will listen to their success-stories and get depressed—lose self-esteem. Even if they try their best to advise you, it won't get through to you. You won't be able to relate to them.

8. Talk to people other people who are having their own setbacks in life

I'm not asking you to talk to just any people. I'm being very specific here: talk to people who are going through bad times as well.

If you start talking to others who are struggling in life, perhaps more so compared to you, then you'll see that everyone else is also having difficulties in life. It will seem natural to you. Moreover, having talked with others might even show you that you are actually doing better than all these other people. You can always find someone who is dealing with more trouble than you and that will enlighten you. That will encourage you. If someone else can deal with tougher setbacks in life, why can't you?

Besides, listening to other people will give you a completely new perspective that you can use for yourself if you ever find yourself in a similar situation as others whom you have talked with.

Conclusion

Setbacks are a part of life. Without them we wouldn't know what the good times are. Without them we wouldn't appreciate the success that we have gotten. Without them we wouldn't cherish the moments that got us to where we are heading to. And without them there wouldn't be any challenge to fill our souls with passion and fire. Take setbacks as a natural process in the journey. Use it to fuel your drive. Use it to move your life forward one step at a time.

Chapter 13:
8 Ways To Gain Self-Confidence

Confidence is not something that can be inherited or learned but is rather a state of mind. Confidence is an attribute that most people would kill to possess. It comes from the feelings of well-being, acceptance of your body and mind (your self-esteem), and belief in your ability, skills, and experience. Positive thinking, knowledge, training, and talking to other people are valuable ways to help improve or boost your confidence levels. Although the definition of self-confidence is different for everyone, the simplest one can be 'to have faith and believe in yourself.'

Here are 8 Ways To Gain More Self-Confidence:

1. **Look at what you have already achieved:**

It's easy to lose confidence when we dwell on our past mistakes and believe that we haven't actually achieved anything yet. It's common to degrade ourselves and not see our achievements as something special. But we should be proud of ourselves even if we do just a single task throughout the day that benefited us or the society in any way. Please make a list of all the things you are proud of, and it can be as small as cleaning your room or as big as getting a good grade or excelling in your job. Keep adding your small or significant achievements every day. Whenever you feel low in confidence, pull out the list and remind yourself how far you have come, how many amazing things you have done, and how far you still have to go.

2. Polish the things you're already good at:

We feel confident in the things we know we are good at. Everyone has some kind of strengths, talents, and skills. You just have to recognize what's yours and work towards it to polish it. Some people are naturally good at everything they do. But that doesn't make you any less unique. You have to try to build on those things that you are good at, and they will help you built confidence in your abilities.

3. Set goals for yourself daily:

Whether it's cooking for yourself, reading a book, studying for a test, planning to meet a friend, or doing anything job-related, make a to-do list for yourself daily. Plan the steps that you have to take to achieve them. They don't necessarily have to be big goals; you should always aim for small achievements. At the end of the day, tick off all the things you did. This will help you gain confidence in your ability to get things done and give you a sense of self-appreciation and self-worth.

4. Talk yourself up:

That tiny voice inside of our heads is the key player in the game of our lives. You'll always be running low on confidence if that voice constantly has negative commentary in your mind telling you that you're not good enough. You should sit somewhere calm and quiet and talk to yourself out of all the negative things. Treat yourself like you would treat a loved one when they tend to feel down. Convince yourself that you can achieve anything, and there's nothing that can stop you. Fill your mind with positive thoughts and act on them.

5. Get a hobby:

Find yourself something that really interests you. It can either be photography, baking, writing, reading, anything at all. When you have found yourself something you are passionate about, commit yourself to it and give it a go. Chances are, you will get motivated and build skills more quickly; this will help you gain self-confidence as you would gradually get better at it and feel accomplished. The praises you will get for it will also boost your confidence.

6. Face your fears:

The best way to gain confidence is to face your fears head-on. There's no time to apply for a promotion or ask someone out on a date until you feel confident enough. Practice facing your fears even if it means that you will embarrass yourself or mess up. Remind yourself that it's just an experiment. You might learn that making mistakes or being anxious isn't half as bad as you would have thought. It will help you gain confidence each time you move forward, and it will prevent you from taking any risks that will result in negative consequences.

7. Surround yourself with positive people:

Observe your friends and the people around you. Do they lift you and accept who you are or bring you down and point out your flaws? A man is known by the company he keeps. Your friends should always positively influence your thoughts and attitude and make you feel better about yourself.

8. Learn To Strike A Balance:

Self-confidence is not a static measure. Some days, we might feel more confident than others. We might often feel a lack of confidence due to criticism, failures, lack of knowledge, or low self-esteem. While another time we might feel over-confident. We might come off as arrogant and self-centred to other people, and it can eventually lead to our failure. We should keep a suitable amount of confidence within ourselves.

Conclusion:

Confidence is primarily the result of how we have been taught and brought up. We usually learn from others how to behave and what to think of ourselves. Confidence is also a result of our experiences and how we learn to react in different situations. Everyone struggles with confidence issues at one time or another, but these quick fixes should enough to boost your confidence. Start with the easier targets, and then work yourself up. I believe in you. Always!

Chapter 14:
What To Do When You Feel Like Your Work is not Good Enough

Feeling like your work is not good enough is very common; your nerves can get better of you at any time throughout your professional life. There is nothing wrong with nerves; It tells you that you care about improving and doing well. Unfortunately, too much nervousness can lead to major self-doubt, and that can be crippling. You are probably very good at your work, and when even once you take a dip, you think that things are not like how they seem to you. If this is something you're feeling, then you're not alone, and this thing is known as Imposter Syndrome. This term is used to describe self-doubt and inadequacy. This one thing leaves people fearing that there might be someone who will expose them. The more pressure you apply to yourself, the more dislocation is likely to occur. You create more anxiety, which creates more fear, which creates more self-doubt. You don't have to continue like this. You can counter it.

Beyond Work

If your imposter syndrome affects you at work, you should take some time out and start focusing on other areas of your life. There are chances that there is something in your personal life that is hindering your work life. This could be anything your sleep routine, friends, diet, or even your relationships. There is a host of external factors that can affect your performance. If there are some boxes you aren't ticking, then there is a high chance of you not performing well at work.

You're Better Than You Think

When you're being crippled by self-doubt, the first thing you have to think about is why you were hired in the first place. The interviewers saw something in you that they believed would improve the business.

So, do you think they would recruit someone who can't do the job? No, they saw your talent, they saw something in you, and you will come good.

When you find yourself in this position, take a moment to write down a few things that you believe led to you being in the role you are now. What did those recruiters see? What did your boss recognize in you? You can also look back on a period of time where you were clicking and felt victorious. What was different then versus now? Was there an external issue like diet, exercise, socializing, etc.?

Check Yourself Before You Wreck Yourself

A checklist might be of some use to you. If you have a list to measure yourself against, then it gives you more than just one thing to judge yourself against. We're far too quick to doubt ourselves and criticize harshly.

The most obvious checklist in terms of work is technical or hard skills, but soft skills matter, too. It's also important to remember that while you're technically proficient now, things move quickly, and you'll reach a point where everything changes, and you have to keep up. You might not ever excel at something, but you can accept the change and adapt to the best of your ability.

It matters that you're hard-working, loyal, honest, and trustworthy. There's more to judge yourself on than just your job. Even if you make a mistake, it's temporary, and you can fix it.

Do you take criticism well? Are you teachable? Easy to coach? Soft skills count for something, which you can look to even at your lowest point and recognize you have strengths.

When you're struggling through a day, week, or even a month, take one large step backward and think about what it is you're unhappy with. What's causing your unhappiness, and how can you improve it?

It comes down to how well you know yourself. If you're clear on what your values are and what you want out of life, then you're going to be fine. If the organization you work for can't respect your values and harness your strengths, then you're better off elsewhere. So, it is extremely important to take time out for that self check-in there could be times you talk to yourself in negative light. Checking in with yourself regularly and not feeding yourself negativity could be one-step forward.

Chapter 15:
8 Ways To Love Yourself First

"Your task is not to seek for love, but merely to seek and find all the barriers within yourself that you have built against it." - Rumi.

Most of us are so busy waiting for someone to come into our lives and love us that we have forgotten about the one person we need to love the most – ourselves. Most psychologists agree that being loved and being able to love is crucial to our happiness. As quoted by Sigmund Freud, "love and work … work and love. That's all there is." It is the mere relationship of us with ourselves that sets the foundation for all other relationships and reveals if we will have a healthy relationship or a toxic one.

Here are some tips on loving yourself first before searching for any kind of love in your life.

1. Know That Self-Love Is Beautiful

Don't ever consider self-love as being narcissistic or selfish, and these are two completely different things. Self-love is rather having positive regard for our wellbeing and happiness. When we adopt self-love, we see higher levels of self-esteem within ourselves, are less critical and harsh with ourselves while making mistakes, and can celebrate our positive qualities and accept all our negative ones.

2. Always be kind to yourself:

We are humans, and humans are tended to get subjected to hurts, shortcomings, and emotional pain. Even if our family, friends, or even our partners may berate us about our inadequacies, we must learn to accept ourselves with all our imperfections and flaws. We look for acceptance from others and be harsh on ourselves if they tend to be cruel or heartless with us. We should always focus on our many positive qualities, strengths, and abilities, and admirable traits; rather than harsh judgments, comparisons, and self-hatred get to us. Always be gentle with yourself.

3. Be the love you feel within yourself:

You may experience both self-love and self-hatred over time. But it would be best if you always tried to focus on self-love more. Try loving yourself and having positive affirmations. Do a love-kindness meditation or spiritual practices to nourish your soul, and it will help you feel love and compassion toward yourself. Try to be in that place of love throughout your day and infuse this love with whatever interaction you have with others.

4. Give yourself a break:

We don't constantly live in a good phase. No one is perfect, including ourselves. It's okay to not be at the top of your game every day, or be happy all the time, or love yourself always, or live without pain. Excuse your bad days and embrace all your imperfections and mistakes. Accept your negative emotions but don't let them overwhelm you. Don't set high standards for yourself, both emotionally and mentally. Don't judge yourself for whatever you feel, and always embrace your emotions wholeheartedly.

5. Embrace yourself:

Are you content to sit all alone because the feelings of anxiety, fear, guilt, or judgment will overwhelm you? Then you have to practice being comfortable in your skin. Go within and seek solace in yourself, practice moments of alone time and observe how you treat yourself. Allow yourself to be mindful of your beliefs, feelings, and thoughts, and embrace solitude. The process of loving yourself starts with understanding your true nature.

6. Be grateful:

Rhonda Bryne, the author of The Magic, advises, "When you are grateful for the things you have, no matter how small they may be, you will see those things instantly increase." Look around you and see all the things that you are blessed to have. Practice gratitude daily and be thankful for all the things, no matter how good or bad they are. You will immediately start loving yourself once you realize how much you have to be grateful for.

7. Be helpful to those around you:

You open the door for divine love the moment you decide to be kind and compassionate toward others. "I slept and dreamt that life was a joy. I awoke and saw that life was service. I acted, and behold, and service was a joy." - Rabindranath Tagore. The love and positive vibes that you wish upon others and send out to others will always find a way back to you. Your soul tends to rejoice when you are kind, considerate, and compassionate. You have achieved the highest form of self-love when you decide to serve others. By helping others, you will realize that you don't need someone else to feel complete; you are complete. It will help you feel more love and fulfillment in your life.

8. Do things you enjoy doing:

If you find yourself stuck in a monotonous loop, try to get some time out for yourself and do the things that you love. There must be a lot of hobbies and passions that you might have put a brake on. Dust them off and start doing them again. Whether it's playing any sport, learning a new skill, reading a new book, writing in on your journal, or simply cooking or baking for yourself, start doing it again. We shouldn't compromise on the things that make us feel alive. Doing the things we enjoy always makes us feel better about ourselves and boost our confidence.

Conclusion:

Loving yourself is nothing short of a challenge. It is crucial for your emotional health and ability to reach your best potential. But the good news is, we all have it within us to believe in ourselves and live the best life we possibly can. Find what you are passionate about, appreciate yourself, and be grateful for what's in your life. Accept yourself as it is.

Chapter 16:
7 Ways On How To Attract Success In Life

Successful people fail more times than unsuccessful people try. A new thought author and metaphysical writer Florence Scovel Shinn in her timeless 1940 novel, 'the secret door to success,' suggests that "Success is not a secret, it is a system." Throughout the centuries, the leaders have alluded to the possibility that success can be attracted into one's life simply by thinking and doing. It is rather a planned journey as we give validity to the premise of creating a plan or setting a goal for ourselves. Goals are set to be achieved, and achievements pave the way for success. Here are 7 Ways To Attract Success In Your Life:

1. **Define What Success Means To You**

Success is subjective to the person who seeks to obtain it, and the ideas may be different for each other. For some of us, success means wealth. For some, it means health and happiness. While for some, it is the mere effort of getting out of bed every day. But the thing that is most highlighted is that we can never get success without struggling. Every one of us wants success, but we do not know how to bring about that life-changing phenomenon that will take us to the zenith of our potential.

2. **Begin with Gratitude:**

From flying to the sky to crashing to the ground, be always thankful to wherever life takes you. Always start by being grateful for what you already have. Whether it's good or bad, we cannot climb the stairs of success without having experiences. If we make mistakes, we should make sure not to give up, rather learn from those mistakes. We must strive to embrace our flaws and imperfections. If we tend to fall seven times, we must have the energy to get up eight times. Whatever life throws us at, no matter the obstacles and challenges, we should always be in a state of gratitude and always be thankful for our learning.

3. Stop making excuses:

Your decisions lead to your destiny. If you are thinking about delaying your work or 'chilling' first, then someone else will take that opportunity for himself. You either grab on the opportunities from both hands, or you sit on the sidelines and watch someone else steal your spotlight. There's no concept of resting and being lazy when you have to work towards your goals and achieve your dreams. One of the major mistakes of unsuccessful people is that they make endless excuses. They would avoid their tasks in any way instead of working on them and actually doing them. You will attract success only if you put your mind towards something and work hard towards it.

4. Realize your potential:

The fine line between incredibly hardworking people and yet fail to achieve success, and the ones who are at the peak of their respective field is simple – potential. We never realize our true potential until we are put in a situation where there's no way out but to express our abilities. We might think that people have more excellent skills than us or have more knowledge than us. But the truth is, we have more potential inside of us. This might be tougher to implement as we don't know how well we can handle things while stressing out or how much hidden talents and skills we possess. Our potential is merely what might make us successful or a failure. It all depends on how much we are willing to try and push ourselves forward.

5. Celebrate the success of others:

What you wish upon others finds its way and comes back to you again. While seeing people being successful in their professional and personal lives and making a fortune in their careers and businesses can be tough on our lives, always remember that they too faced struggles and challenges before reaching here. There's no need to be envious as life has an abundance of everything to offer to everyone. Whatever is it in your destiny will always find its way to you. You can't snatch what others have achieved, and similarly, others can't seize whatever that you have or may achieve. Congratulate people around you and be excited for them. Send out positive vibes to everyone so you may receive the same.

6. Behave as if you are successful:

Have you heard of the term "fake it till you make it?" Well, it applies to this scenario too. You can fake your success and act like a successful person until you really become one. First, surround yourself with lucrative people. See what habits they have developed over time, how they dress up, how they behave, and, most importantly, how much work they do daily to achieve their goals. Get inspired from them and adopt their healthy habits. Be successful in your own eyes first so that eventually you can be successful in other's eyes as well.

7. **Provide value for others:**

While money and fame are the most common success goals, we should first try to focus on creating value in the world. A lot of successful people wanted to change things in the world first and help people out. Mark Zuckerberg built a tool for Harvard students initially and now has over 1.4 billion users. The first thing on our mind after waking up shouldn't be money or success, and it would be to create value for the world and the people around us.

Conclusion:

It would be best if you strived to explore the unique, endless possibilities within you. Then, when you start working on yourself, you're adding to your mind's youth, vitality, and beauty.

Chapter 17: Happy People View Problems as Challenges

To state the obvious: It's easier to be happy when things are going well. Positive outcomes are known to lift people's moods, while negative emotions (like anxiety) generally reflect concerns about negative outcomes.

But, happy people are also good at dealing with problems in ways that help them to maintain their mood, while still dealing with issues effectively. Here are three common things that happy people tend to do to deal with speed bumps in life.

FOCUS ON THE FUTURE

It is important to understand the problem you're facing, and so happy people certainly analyze the situation. But, they don't remain focused on the problem for long. That is, they avoid rumination—which is a set of repeated thoughts about something that has gone wrong.

Instead, they look to the future. There are two benefits to this: One is that the future is not determined yet, and so happy people can be optimistic about things to come. The other is that happy people are looking to make the future better than the past, which creates a hopeful outlook—no matter what the present circumstances look like.

FIND AGENCY

At any given moment, the situation you are in exerts some amount of control over your options. When you're sitting in traffic, for example, there isn't much you can do but wait for the cars around you to start moving. The amount of control you have to take action in a situation is your degree of agency.

Happy people seek out their sources of agency when problems arise. They are most interested in what they can do to influence the situation, rather than focusing on all of the options that have been closed off by what has happened. The focus on agency is important, because it provides the basis for creating a plan to solve the problem. And the sooner a problem is addressed, the less time it has to cause stress.

KNOW WHEN TO FOLD

There are always going to be big problems that you can't solve. Perhaps there is a client who is never satisfied with the work you do. Maybe there is a process you're trying to implement that never seems to have the desired outcome. You might even have been working on the problem for a long time.

Despite all the discussions about the importance of grit, effective (and happy) problem solvers are good at knowing when to walk away from a problem that can't be fixed. Each of us has a limited amount of time and energy that we can devote to the work we are doing. Spending time on problems that cannot be solved has an opportunity cost. There are other things you could be doing with your time that might yield better outcomes. It is important to learn when it is time to give up on a problem rather than continuing to try to solve it.

This is particularly true when you have been working on that problem for a long time. There is a tendency for people to pay attention to sunk costs—the time, money, and energy they have already devoted to working on something. But, those resources are gone, and you can't get them back. If it isn't likely that additional effort is going to help you solve a problem, then you should walk away, no matter how hard you have worked on it already. Happy people are good at ignoring those sunk costs both when making the decision to walk away from a project and after making the decision to walk away. They don't spend time regretting the "wasted" resources.

Chapter 18:
How To Take Action

Today we're going to talk about something pretty crucial. And this also plays into the topics of motivation, purpose, and goals. And that is, "How To Take Action". Before we begin, i want you to write down a couple of things that you were supposed to take action on but have been putting it off for whatever reason. And i want you to keep these things in mind as we go through this video. And hopefully by the end of it, i would have been able to convince you to take action and to start moving forward in your bigger life projects as well.

Why is Taking Action so important? To put it simply, taking action is the one thing that we can control to move us towards our goals. Whether we succeed or not is irrelevant in this case. Many of us hesitate to take action because we are afraid of failure. We fear the unknown and we over analyse and over think things to a point that we become paralysed. And I'm sure you guys have heard this term before: and that is analysis paralysis.

We draw up such detailed plans for how to are going to tackle this problem, we tweak and tweak the draft, aiming to find perfection before we even take the first action step to begin doing the work. And many times, for many people, we just let the plan sit on the shelves or in our computer, afraid to take action because we fear that we might not be able to accomplish the goal we have set out for ourselves.

You see, planning and drafting isn't going to move the needle. When we have a project, planning only makes up a small part of the process. And completion of the project is always down to every member of the group taking action and completing their part of the task. Or in the case of a solo project, all of the action and effort put in comes from you.

When we plan for anything, even for our future, it is something that keeps us in check, to have a reference for us to know that we are on the right track. But whether or not we follow those plans are entirely up to the actions that we actually take. Whether we do save that $100 every month, or not spend money on unnecessary things, or say that we are going to invest in constant education and growth, these are not set in stone if we do not take action.

Another thing that holds us back from taking action is the fear that we will make mistakes. And that we will feel like a fool if we did things wrongly. But if you look at your life, realistically, how many times have you actually done something right the first time around on something that you haven't actually tried before? For example riding a bike, swimming, learning a new language, learning a new instrument. Wouldn't you agree that making mistakes is actually part of the process? Without practice there's not perfect, so why do we think that we will always get it right the first time when it comes to starting a new business or taking action on whatever new thing that we had set our sights on?

We have no problem telling ourselves that making mistakes in smaller things is okay but we berate ourselves or we create this immense expectation that we must get things right the first time around on bigger projects that we fear the climb because we fear the thought of falling down. And we don't even give ourselves a chance to prove that we can do it.

To counter this, we must tell ourselves that making mistakes is a part of the process, to not rush the process, and to give ourselves more room for failure so that we will have the best chance of actually succeeding someday. However long it takes. We must trust the process because it will happen for us eventually. The only time we really do fail is the last time we actually stop trying, stop taking action, and stop learning from our mistakes. that is the time when we can say we are a failure, if we quit. But if we never give up, and we keep taking action, it will work out for us.

One final hurdle that many of us face is that we tend to want to rush the process and we set unrealistic deadlines to achieve those goals. If we go back to our previous example of learning a new instrument, how many of you guys will agree that, although not impossible, it is unrealistic to become a guitar guru after the 1st year? Most of us would realistically say that it will take at least a few years of daily practice to actually become a pro guitar player. But how many of us actually apply that same concept to a big project like growing our income from $3k to $10k. We all expect fast results and fast growth, but rarely does things work out so smoothly, unless we are incredibly lucky.

When we set these big targets but fail to realise that we need to take baby steps consistently everyday, we set ourselves up for failure without realising it. Without giving ourselves the room to grow a seed into a tree, we end up chopping it down when it is still at the early growth stages. And we fail to let time and effort do it's thing, giving it water and light day in and day out. And we beat ourselves up when we quit prematurely.

What I have learnt, from experience, is that the best way to achieve something eventually, is to take baby steps, taking a little action each day, be it 5 mins, an hour, or 10 hours, they all count. And instead of just hoping to rush to the end, that I actually learned to not only enjoy the process, but also to trust that my efforts will all pay off in the end. And many a times, they did. I left the fear and worry to one side and just focused on taking action. I stopped comparing myself with my peers, and focused on my own journey. I can't control how much faster my competition can grow or achieve, but i can definitely control my own destiny.

So i challenge each and everyone of you today to take a look at the list of things that you hope to achieve that you have written down at the start of this video, and to take the first step of stop trying to perfect the plan, to stop thinking and worrying about what might and could go wrong, to stop fearing the unknown, and to simply just take a little action each day. The worse thing that you can do to yourself is to not even try. You will make mistakes along the way, but as long as you learn from them, you will be moving in the right direction.

Chapter 19:
Creating Successful Habits

Successful people have successful habits.

If you're stuck in life, feeling like you're not going anywhere, take a hard look at your habits.

Success is built from our small daily habits accumulated together, Without these building blocks, you will not get far in life.

Precise time management, attention to detail, these are the traits of all who have made it big.

To change your life, you must literally change your life, the physical actions and the mindset.

Just as with success, the same goes with health.

Do you have the habit of a healthy diet and regular athletic exercises?

Healthy people have healthy habits.

If you are unhappy about your weight and figure, point the finger at your habits once again.

To become healthy, happy and wealthy, we must first become that person in the mind.

Success is all psychological.

Success has nothing to do with circumstances.

Until we have mastered the habits of our thinking we cannot project this success on the world.

We must first decide clearly who we want to be.
We must decide what our values are.
We must decide what we want to achieve.
Then we must discipline ourselves to take control of our destiny.

Once we know who we are and what we want to do,
Behaving as if it were reality becomes easy.

We must start acting the part.
That is the measure of true faith.
We must act as if we have already succeeded.
As the old saying goes: "fake it UNTIL YOU MAKE IT"

Commit yourself with unwavering faith.
Commit yourself with careful and calculated action.
You will learn the rest along the way

Every habit works towards your success or failure,
No matter how big or how small.
The more you change your approach as you fail, the better your odds become.
Your future life will be the result of your actions today.
It will be positive or negative depending on your actions now.

You will attain free-will over your thoughts and actions.
The more you take control, the happier you will be.

Guard your mind from negativity.
Your mind is your sanctuary.
Ignore the scaremongering.
Treat your mind to pure motivation.

We cannot avoid problems.
Problems are a part of life.
Take control of the situation when it arises.
Have a habit of responding with action rather than fear.

Make a habit of noticing everybody and respecting everybody.
Build positive relationships and discover new ideas.
Be strong and courageous, yet gentle and reasonable.
These are the habits of successful leaders.

Be meticulous.
Be precise.
Be focused.

Make your bed in the morning.
Follow the path of drill sergeants in the royal marines and US navy seals.
Simple yet effective,
This one habit will shift your mindset first thing as you greet the new day.

Choose to meditate.
Find a comfortable place to get in touch with your inner-self.
Make it a habit to give yourself clarity of the mind and spirit.
Visualize your goals and make them a reality in your mind.

Choose to work in a state of flow.
Be full immersed in your work rather than be distracted.
To be productive we need to have an incredible habit of staying focused.
It will pay off.
It will pay dividends.
The results will be phenomenal.

Every single thing you choose to make a habit will add up.
No matter how big or how small,
Choose wisely.

Choose the habit of treating others with respect.
Treat the cleaner the same as you would with investors and directors.
Treat the poor the same as you would with the CEO of a multi-national company.
Our habits and attitude towards ourselves and others makes up our character.

Choose a habit of co-operation over competition,
After all the only true competition is with ourselves.

It doesn't matter whether someone is doing better than us as long as we are getting better.
If someone is doing better we should learn from them.
Make it a habit of putting ourselves into someone else's shoes.
We might stand to learn a thing or two.

No habit is too big or too small.
To be happy and successful we must do our best in them all.

Chapter 20:
Overcoming the Fear of Failure

Stop it.

Stop whatever you are doing and take a moment to listen because you need to hear this...

Right now I want you to close your eyes and remember a time that you failed. I want you to remember how it made you feel. Remember the pain. Remember the guilt. Dig deep and remember the crushing weight of DISAPPOINTMENT that dragged you down to the depths of hell.

Do you feel it?! DO YOU REMEMBER THAT FEELING?! Good. Now get used to it - because you're gonna feel it again.

I need you to understand that failure is a part of life. In fact it's more than that. It's an essential part of life, of success! You think winners never failed? You think it's just you? Winners have failed more times than losers have ever TRIED!

People who succeed don't stop when they fail. They don't stop at ten, fifty or a hundred failures! They push through. They persevere. It doesn't matter how many times they get knocked down. They get right back up. Again. And again. And again. You know why? They don't fear failure.

Listen closely, because this will change your life. So long as you fear failure, you will never achieve success. You will never reach your dreams. Fearing failure is the only thing stopping you from becoming great. Greatness is a title reserved only for those who are willing to go head to head with failure - for those who face the fear of failure without hesitation! They look failure in the eye and say "I'll be damned if I let YOU sat and in my way!"

When they asked Michael Jordan how many shots he made, you know what he said? He told them they were nothing compared to how many he missed. Michael Jordan became the greatest basketball player of all time because he wasn't afraid to fail! What do you think would have happened if he had given up? If he had been scared to fail. He would never have become the legend that he did. He would have stayed a nobody - just like you.

Did that hurt? How did it make you feel? The pain. The guilt. The disappointment of knowing that so long as you fear failure YOU WILL BE A NOBODY. Your talent, your ability, the greatness within you! They will all die within you. If you aren't ready to accept that, then you need to make a change.

Get up. Get up from wherever you are hiding and face failure one on one. That fear is the only thing standing between you and success. You've got to get it through your head that this is it, the moment of truth. This is the time to decide who you are. Either you are a winner or a loser. If you can't look failure in the eye to achieve your dreams then you will never rise beyond mediocrity. But if you are a winner, now is the time to prove it. Forget mediocrity, you rise to the occasion. Failure is nothing more than one step closer to the greatness you desire. And if you can do that, if you can overcome the fear of failure... you can do anything.

Chapter 21:
Why You Are Amazing

When was the last time you told yourself that you were amazing? Was it last week, last month, last year, or maybe not even once in your life?

As humans, we always seek to gain validation from our peers. We wait to see if something that we did recently warranted praise or commendation. Either from our colleagues, our bosses, our friends, or even our families. And when we don't receive those words that we expect them to, we think that we are unworthy, or that our work just wasn't good enough. That we are lousy and under serving of praise.

With social media and the power of the internet, these feelings have been amplified. For those of us that look at the likes on our Instagram posts or stories, or the number of followers on Tiktok, Facebook, or Snapchat, we allow ourselves to be subjected to the validation of external forces in order to qualify our self-worth. Whether these are strangers who don't know you at all, or whoever they might be, their approval seems to matter the most to us rather than the approval we can choose to give ourselves.

We believe that we always have to up our game in order to seek happiness. Everytime we don't get the likes, we let it affect our mood for the rest of the day or even the week.

Have you ever thought of how wonderful it is if you are your best cheerleader in life? If the only validation you needed to seek was from yourself? That you were proud of the work you put out there, even if the world disagrees, because you know that you have put your heart and soul into the project and that there was nothing else you could have done better in that moment when you were producing that thing?

I am here to tell you that you are amazing because only you have the power to choose to love yourself unconditionally. You have the power to tell yourself that you are amazing. and that you have the power to look into yourself and be proud of how far you came in life. To be amazed by the things that you have done up until this point, things that other people might not have seen, acknowledged, or given credit to you for. But you can give that credit to yourself. To pat yourself on the back and say "I did a great job".

I believe that we all have this ability to look inwards. That we don't need external forces to tell us we are amazing because deep down, we already know we are.

If nobody else in the world loves you, know that I do. I love your courage, your bravery, your resilience, your heart, your soul, your commitment, and your dedication to live out your best life on this earth. Tell yourself each and everyday that you deserve to be loved, and that you are loved.

Go through life fiercely knowing that you don't need to seek happiness, validations, and approval from others. That you have it inside you all along and that is all you need to keep going.

Chapter 22:
Discovering Your Purpose

If you guys don't already know, this is one of the topics that I really love talking about. And I never get tired of it. Having a purpose is something that I always believe everyone should have. Having a purpose to live, to breathe, to get up each day, I believe that without purpose, there is no point to life.

So today we're going to talk about how to discover your purpose, and why you should make it a point to find one if you didn't already start looking.

So what is purpose exactly. A purpose is a reason to do something. Is to have something else greater than ourselves to work for. You see, I believe if we are only focused on ourselves, instead of others, we will not be able to be truly happy in life. Feeding our own self interests does not bring us joy as one might think. After living the life that I had, I realized that true happiness only comes when you bring joy to someone else's life. Whether it be helping others professionally or out of selflessness, this happiness will radiate and reflect back to us from someone else who is appreciative of your efforts.

On some level, we can look into ourselves to be happy. For example being grateful for life, loving ourselves, and all that good stuff. Yes keep doing those things. But there is a whole other dimension if we devote our time and energy into helping others once we have already conquered ourselves. If you look at many of the most successful people on the planet, after they have acquired an immense amount of wealth, many of them look to passion projects or even philanthropy where they can give back to the community when having more money doesn't do anything for them anymore. If you look at Elon Musk and Jeff Bezos, these two have a greater purpose which is their space projects. Where they visualise humans being able to move out of Earth one day where civilisation is able to expand. Or Bill Gates and Warren Buffet, who have pledged to give billions of their money away for philanthropic work, to help the less fortunate and to fund organisations that work towards finding cures to diseases.

Now for us mere mortals, we don't need to think so big. Our purpose need not be so extravagant. It can be as simple as having a purpose to provide for your loved one, to work hard to bring your family members of holidays and travel, or to bring joy to your elderly relatives by organising activities for them to do. There is no purpose that is too big or too small.

Your purpose could be helping others find a beautiful home, doing charitable work, or even feeding and providing for your growing family.

As humans, we will automatically work harder if we have a clear and defined purpose. We have a reason to get up each day, to go to work, to earn that paycheck, so that we can spend it on things and people, even ourselves at times. Without a purpose, we struggle to find meaning in the work that we do. We struggle to see the big picture and we find that we have no reason to work so hard, or even at all. And we struggle to find life worth living.

This revelation came to me when I started seeing my work as helping some other person in a meaningful way. Where my work was not just about making money to buy nice things, but to be able to impact someone else's life in a positive way. That became my purpose. To see them learn something new, and to bring a joy and smile to their faces. That thought that I was contributing something useful to someone made me smile more than money ever could. Yes money can help you live a comfortable life, but helping others can go a much farther way into giving your life true purpose.

So I challenge each and everyone of you to find a purpose in everything that you do, and if you struggle to find one, start by making the goal to help others a priority. Think of the difference you can make to others and that could very well be your purpose in life as well.

Chapter 23:
Happy People Don't Hold on To Grudges

Holding a grudge is when you harbor anger, bitterness, resentment, or other negative feelings long after someone has done something to hurt you. Usually, it's in response to something that's already occurred. Other times a grudge may develop after simply perceiving that someone is against you or means you harm—whether or not they do. Grudges also often feature persistent rumination about the person and/or incident at the center of your ill-will.

While we don't often like to admit it, holding a grudge is a common way some people respond to the feeling that they've been wronged. If you're still mad well after a precipitating incident, you may be holding on to those negative feelings for too long, sometimes well after other people typically would have let them go. You may remember multiple past bad acts and relive those experiences every time you think about or interact with that person—either making your displeasure abundantly clear to them or keeping your true feelings to yourself. You might be intentionally holding a grudge, but sometimes you aren't even aware of it.

But whatever your intentions or the cause of your bitterness, holding a grudge can end up hurting you as much as the person who inspired it. Learn more about how clinging to anger can impact you emotionally, physically, and socially, as well as how to begin to let go of your grudges and cope with anger more healthily. From early childhood on, holding a grudge is one-way people respond to negative feelings and events. This reaction is particularly common when you think someone has done something intentionally, callously, or thoughtlessly to hurt you, especially if they don't seem to care or make an attempt to apologize or make the situation right.

If you have low self-esteem, poor coping skills, were embarrassed by the hurt, and/or have a short temper, you may be even more likely to hold a grudge. While we all may fall into holding an occasional grudge, some people may be more prone to hanging on to resentments or anger than other people. Sometimes, holding grudges—and blaming others—may be a form of self-protection. In the same vein, some people may be more conscious that they are stoking feelings of bitterness than others, which may be unaware of their role in keeping their anger alive. Lasting bitterness can grow from a variety of issues—large and small—as well.

Chapter 24:
Showing Up

Today we are going to talk about the simple concept of "Showing Up". And this is going to touch on the topic of motivation as well.

You see for many of us who struggle with laziness and a lack of willpower, we wait for inspiration to strike, or the perfect storm of feeling good and motivated before we make the effort to hit the hit or start taking action on the task that we have been putting off. We think that we need to be all pumped up and excited before doing anything, but many a times, these feelings are few and they rarely come when we expect them to.

There are days where I would plan a gym session only to cancel because I didn't feel like it. And there are times when I would plan a meetup with my friends only to feel lazy at the last second and cancelling. And there are also times when I plan to work at a particular cafe but decided against it because I was too tired.

All these moments where I lacked the willpower to get things started or keeping to my word only made my future commitments even more vulnerable to default. As i was giving in to my desires to be lazy, the next time it came around the excuses became easier and easier to justify. And that only led to a less favourable outcome with regards to my mental, physical, and emotional health. I was spiraling to a life of mediocrity every time i let my inner demon win.

This all changed when I came across an article that said that all you needed to do was to show up for your activity, even if u didn't want to. Just to do a quick 5 min session rather than a long 1 hour session that i would normally have planned out. Or to simply just get to the desk to work for 15mins rather than the 5 hours I would normally have set aside time to do.

I found that by the simple act of showing up for my activity, I had given myself the best possible chance to fulfilling that promise to myself. At the gym, one rep turned into 10 reps, and 5 mins of workout turned into a 2 hour one as i told myself you can do one more, and one more after that. And as I watched people workout around me, i felt motivated to put in more effort in my workout as well. This simple change made it easier for me to simply show up the next day at the gym and let the process play out on its own once again. The same principle came to work and play. I realised that all i needed to do was to get out of the house and the rest would take care of itself. To show up at my desk and gym, no matter how late I may be, that at least when I am there, I will begin the task one way or another.

I challenge each and everyone of you to give it a try. If you find the task that you dread to be too daunting, that Instead of setting a specific time that you need to spend on it, that you simply just show up. And let your body dictate how much time you should indeed spend on that activity.

Be it 5 mins or 5 hours. I have found that once I start something that it takes a lot of energy for me to stop. It is like a moving train or car, that once u get going you will most probably go till you can't go no more. Then you slowly grind to a halt and show up for the next activity.

Chapter 25:
Enjoying The Simple Things

Today we're going to talk about a topic that might sound cheesy, but trust me it's worth taking a closer look at. And that is how we should strive to enjoy the simple things in life.

Many of us think we need a jam packed schedule for the week, month, or year, to tell us that we are leading a very productive and purposeful life. We find ways to fill our time with a hundred different activities. Going to this event, that event, never slowing down. And we find ourselves maybe slightly burnt out by the end of it.

We forget that sometimes simplicity is better than complication. Have you sat down with your family for a simple lunch meal lately? You don't have to talk, you just have to be in each other's company and enjoying the food that is being served in front of you.

I found myself appreciating these moments more than I did running around to activities thinking that I needed something big to be worth my time. I found sitting next to my family on the couch watching my own shows while they watch theirs very rewarding. I found eating alone at my favourite restaurant while watching my favourite sitcom to be equally as enjoyable as hanging out with a group of 10 friends. I also found myself richly enjoying a long warm shower every morning and evening. It is the highlights of my day.

My point is that we need to start looking at the small things we can do each day that will bring us joy. Things that are within our control. Things that we know can hardly go wrong. This will provide some stability to gain some pleasure from. The little nuggets in the day that will not be determined by external factors such as the weather, friends bailing on us, or irritating customers.

When we focus on the little things, we make life that much better to live through.

Chapter 26:
10 Reasons Money Can't Buy You Happiness

I'm sure you have heard this statement before, that "Money can't buy happiness.", but have you stopped to think about why it might be so? Many of us chase money and that high paying job because we believe that it will bring us wealth which will in turn make us happy. We do it because it is what society tells us we should be doing. That we should trade all our time and energy to make money no matter how many sacrifices we have to make with regards to our friendships, relationships, and so on.

It is true that a certain income level and money in the bank is required to allow us to have a comfortable standard of living, which could make life quite nice for us. But beyond that, it will be tough to derive happiness from just sheer truckloads of money alone, as we will soon find out.

1. Our Happiness Is Not Derived From Material Things

This is arguably the most important yet easily overlooked aspect when it comes to dealing with money. While most of us will have desires to live in a dream home, owning the ultimate luxury car, and buying the greatest gifts we can buy when we're rich, we fail to realize that the process of acquisition of material things is a futile effort. It is always thrilling to be on the forefront of owning the latest material good on the market, but the excitement you have for a product usually fades away pretty quickly once you have them in your hands. We acclimatize very quickly to what we have, and we search for the next thing almost immediately. This seemingly endless chase for happiness would seem like a carrot on a stick, always dangling it's juiciness in front of you but you never get to taste it. If you look around at the things you have in your house, you will know what I mean. All the stuff that was once intriguing to you now no longer has the same effect of joy and happiness that it once had. Bottom line is that there is no amount of stuff you can acquire that will ever make you truly happy.

2. Money Cannot Buy You Relationships

We fail to realize the power of relationships when it comes to the happiness equation. Happiness can easily be derived from thriving relationships. Relationships that serve to enrich our lives in all aspects of it. When we are in a relationship with someone who loves and cares for us unconditionally, there is no amount of money that can buy you that feeling. The same goes for friendships and family. Having people that support you in your endeavors, grieve with you when you experience loss, or just someone you can talk to, to share your feelings of excitement, sorrow, and all the different ranges of emotions, those are the moments that truly matter in life.

3. Money Could Lure Disingenuous People

While some may argue that you can buy friendships by paying people to be around you, I am pretty sure most of you wouldn't want to go down that path. You know that these people are not hanging around you because they like you, but because they like what you have in your pocket. Genuine relationships are ones that will last even when you don't have a dime left in your back account. When all else fails, you will want to have these people around you for support.

4. You Will Never Feel Like You have Enough Money

Chasing money as a substitute for happiness is a tricky thing. We all think we need $1 million dollars in our bank account to be happy, but as soon as we hit that milestone, something just doesn't feel quite right. We feel empty inside, we feel like maybe it's not enough, so we set a bigger target of $2 million. But that day will come too and again we will feel like something is amiss. The cycle repeats itself until we finally realize that deriving happiness from a monetary goal is also a futile effort.

5. Money Only Helps To Improve Your Standard of Living

Instead of using money as bait for happiness, use it for what it really is for - survival, food, clothing, a roof over your head, and the occasional splurge on something you like. Beyond that, look elsewhere for happiness. I am here to tell you that it is human nature for us to feel like we never have enough of something, and that includes money. We have been programmed to always want and need more. More of everything. We compare to people more successful than us and think we need to live like them in order to be happy. Don't make the same mistake as everyone else. Find a comfortable amount you need for survival and retirement, and the rest is bonus.

6. Making Money Requires Sacrifices

Unless you're a trust fund baby, or money falls from the sky, or you managed to strike a jackpot, constantly putting money above all else requires time and effort to earn. Working 12 hour shifts, 7 days a week is no easy feat. You will see your youth fly by and your other priorities fall by the wayside. By the time you've earned the desired income of your dreams, you may well find that a few decades have passed and you're standing on top of the mountain, alone, with no one to share that experience with. No one who may be able to travel with you or even spend that money with you. Unless you consciously try for a balanced work-life, you will find it quite a lonesome experience.

7. The Simple Pleasures In Life Doesn't Require That Much Money

Spending time with your family, going out for coffee with friends, having a chill board games night on the weekends with enthusiasts like yourself, you will find that all these activities brings us closer to the emotional world. The emotional and spiritual connection we have with fellow human beings that bring us laughter, joy, sadness, and happiness. We fail to realize that the happiest moments we can create doesn't require that much money. It just requires planning and some food. Stop chasing the dream vacation halfway around the world for happiness. It is underneath you all along.

8. You Lack the Happiness Mindset

Happiness is merely a feeling, and feelings can be created by choice. Money can't fix your emotional problems, it can only buy you therapy. Ultimately, it's your attitude and mindset that determines your level of happiness that you experience. If you always see the glass half empty, no amount of money can make you see the glass as half full.

9. You Don't Feel Grateful for The Things Money Buy You

We take for granted the things we have acquired so far and only look towards the next shiny object. Being grateful for our hard-earned money has bought us thus far should be our number one priority. Treasure the bed you bought that you can sleep comfortably in, be thankful for the television you have that allows you to stream your favourite shows on demand, be grateful for the roof that houses all these items and protects you from the elements.

10. We Fall into The If-Then Trap of Chasing Money

How many times do you have the thought that the next promotion you receive will be the happiest moment of your life. Or perhaps that your boss will give me a raise if you turn this project in successfully. If we only chase our paychecks rather than chase fulfillment, we are running the wrong race in life.

Remember these important points the next time you work for money. Yes, having money is important, but it should not adversely affect your ability to live a fulfilling life. There are a million other things that are just as equally important if you're chasing happiness.

Chapter 27:
6 Steps To Focus On Growth

Growth is a lifelong process. We grow every moment from the day we are born until our eventual death. And the amazing thing about growth is that there is no real limit to it.

Now, what exactly is growth? Well, growing is the process of changing from one state to another and usually, it has to be positive; constructive; better-than-before. Although growth occurs equally towards all directions in the early years of our life, the rate of growth becomes more and more narrowed down to only a few particular aspects of our life as we become old. We become more distinctified as individuals, and due to our individuality, not everyone of us can possibly grow in all directions. With our individual personality, experiences, characteristics, our areas of growth become unique to us. Consequently, our chances of becoming successful in life corresponds to how we identify our areas of growth and beam them on to our activities with precision. Let us explore some ways to identify our key areas of growth and utilize them for the better of our life.

1. **Identify Where You Can Grow**

For a human being, growth is relative. One person cannot grow in every possible way because that's how humans are—we simply cannot do every thing at once. One person may grow in one way while another may grow in a completely different way. Areas of growth can be so unlike that one's positive growth might even seem like negative growth to another person's perspective. So, it is essential that we identify the prime areas where we need to grow. This can be done through taking surveys, asking people or critically analyzing oneself. Find out what lackings do you have as a human being, find out what others think that you lack as a human being. Do different things and note down where you are weak but you have to do it anyway. Then, make a list of those areas where you need growing and move on to the next step.

2. **Accept That You Need To Grow In Certain Areas**

After carefully identifying your lackings, accept these in your conscious and subconscious mind. Repeatedly admit to yourself and others that you lack so and so qualities where you wish to grow with time.

Never feel ashamed of your shortcomings. Embrace them comfortably because you cannot trully change yourself without accepting that you need to change. Growth is a dynamic change that drags you way out of your comfort zone and pushes you into the wild. And to start on this endeavor for growth, you need to have courage. Growth is a choice that requires acceptance and humility.

3. Remind Yourself of Your Shortcomings

You can either write it down and stick it on your fridge or just talk about it in front of people you've just met—this way, you'll constantly keep reminding yourself that you have to grow out of your lackings. And this remembrance will tell you to try—try improving little by little. Try growing.

It is important to remain consciously aware of these at all times because you never know when you might have to face what. All the little and big things you encounter every day are all opportunities of growth. This takes us to the fourth step:

4. Face Your Problems

Whatever you encounter, in any moment or place in your life is an opportunity created: an opportunity for learning. A very old adage goes: "the more we learn, the more we grow". So, if you don't face your problems and run away from them, then you are just losing the opportunity to learn from it, and thus, losing the opportunity of growing from it. Therefore, facing whatever life throws at you also has an important implication on your overall growth. Try to make yourself useful against all odds. Even if you fail at it, you will grow anyway.

5. Cross The Boundary

So, by now you have successfully identified your areas of growth, you have accepted them, you constantly try to remind yourself of them and you face everything that comes up, head on—never running away. You are already making progress. Now comes the step where you push yourself beyond your current status. You go out of what you are already facing and make yourself appear before even more unsettling circumstances.

This is a very difficult process, but if you grow out of here, nothing can stop you ever. And only a few people successfully make it through. You create your own problems, no one might support you and yet still, you try to push forward, make yourself overcome new heights of difficulties and grow like the tallest tree in the forest. You stand out of the crowd. This can only be done in one or two subjects in a lifetime. So make sure that you know where you want to grow. Where you want to invest that much effort, and time, and dedication. Then, give everything to it. Growth is a life's journey.

6. Embrace Your Growth

After you have crossed the boundary, there is no turning back. You have achieved new heights in your life, beyond what you thought you could have ever done. The area—the subject in which you tried to develop yourself, you have made yourself uniquely specialized in that particular area. You have outgrown the others in that field. It is time for you to make yourself habituated with that and embrace it gracefully. The wisdom you've accumulated through growth is invaluable—it has its roots deeply penetrated into your life. The journey that you've gone through while pursuing your growth will now define you. It is who you are.

As I've mentioned in the first line, "growth is a lifelong process". Growth is not a walk in the park, It is you tracking through rough terrains—steep heights and unexplored depths for an entire lifetime. Follow these simple yet difficult steps; grow into the tallest tree and your life will shine upon you like the graceful summer sun.

Chapter 28:

Be Motivated by Challenge

You have an easy life and a continuous stream of income, you are lucky! You have everything you and your children need, you are lucky! You have your whole future planned ahead of you and nothing seems to go in the other direction yet, you are lucky!

But how far do you think this can go? What surety can you give yourself that all will go well from the start to the very end?

Life will always have a hurdle, a hardship, a challenge, right there when you feel most satisfied. What will you do then?

Will you give up and look for an escape? Will you seek guidance? Or will you just give up and go down a dark place because you never thought something like this could happen to you?

Life is full of endless possibilities and an endless parade of challenges that make life no walk in the park.

You are different from any other human being in at least one attribute. But your life isn't much different than most people's. You may be less fortunate or you may be the luckiest, but you must not back down when life strikes you.

This world is a cruel place and a harsh terrain. But that doesn't mean you should give up whenever you get hit in the back. That doesn't mean you don't catch what the world throws at you.

Do you know what you should do? Look around and observe for examples. Examples of people who have had the same experiences as you had and what good or bad things did they do? You will find people on both extremes.

You will find people who didn't have the courage or guts to stand up to the challenge and people who didn't have the time to give up but to keep pushing harder and harder, just to get better at what they failed the last time.

The challenges of life can never cross your limits because the limits of a human being are practically infinite. But what feels like a heavy load, is just a shadow of your inner fear dictating you to give up.

But you can't give up, right? Because you already have what you need to overcome this challenge too. You just haven't looked into your backpack of skills yet!

If you are struggling at college, go out there and prove everyone in their wrong. Try to get better grades by putting in more hours little by little.

If people take you as a non-social person, try to talk to at least one new person each day.

If you aren't getting good at a sport, get tutorials and try to replicate the professionals step by step and put in all your effort and time if you truly care for the challenge at hand.

The motivation you need is in the challenge itself. You just need to realize the true gains you want from each stone in your path and you will find treasures under every stone.

Chapter 29:
Consistency can bring you happiness.

Happiness is an individual concept.
One man's riches is another man's rubbish.
As humans we are not happy if we do not have a routine, a reason to get up, and a purpose to live.

Without working towards something consistently, we become lost.
We begin to drift.
Drifting with no purpose eventually leads to emptiness.

When we are drifting in a job we hate,
We are trading our future away,
When we inconsistent in our relationships,
Problems are bound to arise.

Choose consistent focus instead.
Figure out exactly what you want and start to change it.
Employ consistent routines and habits that to move you towards your goals.

Consistency and persistence are key to success and happiness.
Without consistent disciplined effort towards what we want, we resign to a life of mediocrity.

Read a book for an hour consistently every single day.
You will become a national expert in 1 year.
In 5 years, a global expert.
That is the power of consistency.
Instead, people spend most of their free time scrolling through social media.

Consistency starts in the mind.
Control your thoughts to be positive despite the circumstances.
Nothing in the world can make us happy if we choose not to be.

Choose to be happy now and consistently working towards your goals.
We cannot be happy and successful if we dwell in the day to day setbacks.

We must consistently move like a bulldozer.
We have to keep going no matter what.
Nothing stays in the path of a bulldozer for too long.

In life, no matter where you are, you only ever have two choices.
Choose to stay where you are? Or choose to keep moving?

If where you are is making you happy, then by all means do more of it.
If not. What will? And why?
This should be clear before you take action.
Start with the end in your mind.
Let your body catch-up to it afterwards.

The end result is your what.
The action required is your how.
Concentrate on the what and the how and it will all be revealed soon enough.

Concentrate consistently on what you want for yourself and your family.
Distraction and lack of consistent action is a killer of happiness and success.
Your happiness is the life you want.
Take consistent action towards that life you've always dreamed of.
Commitment and endurance is part of that process.

On earth things need time to nurture and grow.
Everything in life depends on it.
The right conditions for maximum growth.

You can't just throw a seed on the concrete and expect it to grow with no soil and water,
Just as you can't simply wish for change and not create the right environment for success.

A seed requires not just consistent sunlight,
But the perfect combination of water and nutrients as well.
You might have given that seed sunlight,
just as you have your dream hope,
But without faith and consistent action towards the goal, nothing will happen.

The seed will still stay a seed forever.

Consistency in thought and action is everything towards happiness.
Nothing can grow without it.
Your success can be measured by your time spent working towards your goals.
If we consistently do nothing we become successful in nothing.
If we have to do something, should it not be something worth doing?

Start doing things that make you happy and fulfilled.
Consistency towards something that makes you happy is key towards lasting success.
Adapt when necessary but remain consistent with the end result in mind.
The path can be changed when necessary but the destination cannot.
Accepting anything less is admitting defeat.

Consistent concentration on the end result can and will be tested.
It however cannot be defeated, unless you quit.
If we remain steadfast in our belief that this is possible for us, it will be possible.
After a while things will seem probable. Eventually it becomes definite.

Continue to believe you can do it despite the circumstances.
Continue despite everyone around you saying you can't do it.

In spite of social status,
in spite of illness or disability,

in spite of age, race or nationality,

know you can do nearly anything if you consistently put all of your mind and body towards the task.

Take the pressure off.

There is no set guideline.

It is what you make of it.

There is no set destination or requirements.

Those are set my you.

The only competition is yourself from yesterday.

If you can consistently outperform that person, your success is guaranteed.

Consistent concentration and action towards your dream is key you your success and happiness.

Chapter 30:
Enjoying The Journey

Today I want to talk about why enjoying the journey of life is important. And why hurrying to get to the destination might not be all that enjoyable as we think it is.

A lot of us plan our lives around an end goal, whether it be getting to a particular position in our company's ladder, or becoming the best player in a sport, or having the most followers on Instagram or whatever the goal may be... Many of us just can't wait to get there. However, many a times, once we reach our goal, whilst we may feel a sense of satisfaction and accomplishment for a brief moment, we inevitably feel like something is missing again and we search for our next objective and target to hit.

I have come to realise that in life, it is not always so much the end goal, but the journey, trials, struggles, and tribulations that make the journey there worth it. If we only focus on the end goal, we may miss out the amazing sights along the way. We will ultimately miss the point of the journey and why we embarked on it in the first place.

Athletes who achieve one major title never stop at just that one, they look for the next milestone they can achieve, but they enjoy the process, they take it one step at a time and at the end of their careers they can look back with joy that they had left no stone unturned. And that they can live their life without regret.

How many times have you seen celebrities winning the biggest prize in their careers, whether it may be the Grammy's Album of the Year if you are a musician, or the Oscars Best Actor or Best Actress Award. How many of them actually feel like that is the end of the journey? They keep creating and keep making movies and film not because they want that award, even though it is certainly a nice distinction to have, but more so because they enjoy their craft and they enjoy the art of producing.

If winning that trophy was the end goal, we would see many artists just end their careers there and then after reaching the summit. However that is not the case. They will try to create something new for as long as people are engaged with their craft, as with the case of Meryl Streep, even at 70+ she is still working her butt off even after she has achieve all the fame and money in the world.

Even for myself, at times i just want to reach the end as quickly as possible. But many times when i get there, i am never satisfied. I feel empty inside and i feel that I should be doing more. And when i rush to the end, i do feel like I missed many important sights along the way that would have made the journey much more rewarding and enjoyable had I told myself to slow it down just a little.

I believe that for all of us, the journey is much more important than the destination. It is through the journey that we grow as a person, it is through the journey that we evolve and take on new ideas, work ethics, knowledge, and many little nuggets that make the trip worth it at the end. If someone were to hand you a grand slam title without having you earned it, it would be an empty trophy with no meaning and emotions behind it. The trophy would not represent the hours of hard work that you have put in to be deserving of that title.

So I challenge each and everyone of you today to take a step back in whatever journey you may be on. To analyse in what aspects can you enjoy the moment and to not place so much pressure into getting to the destination asap. Take it one day at a time and see how the journey you are on is actually a meaningful one that you should treasure each day and not let up.

Chapter 31:

"Happy People Enjoy the Hidden Pleasures life has to offer."

It is said that the best things in your life are free, and there is not even a shred of doubt in that life is filled with satisfying hidden pleasures. To feel fulfilled, you need to enjoy them, so we are going to list some of the most simple, satisfying hidden pleasures life has to offer so that next time when you find yourself in a similar situation, you take out a moment and truly enjoy it:

Finding money you did not know you had: Reaching into your pocket and finding out a dollar 20 bill from the last time you went out wearing those jeans brings absolute joy all of a sudden. You have some extra money on you that you completely forgot about.

Receiving a Real letter via snail mail: Since email is more used these days, it has become the primary source of written communication, and most of the things you find in your snail mail are junk. So, when you find a package or a letter from someone you know in the mail, it brings joy, and a sense of excitement takes over you as you start opening the gift.

Making Brief Eye Contact with Someone of the Opposite Sex: We are all so busy in our lives, and most of the times when we are out, we spend time looking at our screens, so sometimes there is a rare moment where you pass them in a subway or street, and they look at you momentarily making direct eye contact that communicates a subtle curiosity, and for a second you think about it and then it's just gone.

Saying the Same Thing Simultaneously: Sometimes, you and your friend notice something or react to something by yelling out the same set of words. This is something that occurs rarely, but it gives you something to smile about.

Realizing You Have More Time to Sleep: Sometimes, you abruptly wake up in the middle of the night, and you think it's time to wake up, and when you look at the time, and you still have two more hours to sleep. A warm euphoric feeling shoots through your body at that moment, and then you glide back to your dreams.

The feeling after a healthy workout: There is a feeling of self-satisfaction and accomplishment that you get; this is one activity that will make you feel better and also make you look good at the same time. So when you walk out of the main door of the gym, you feel like you are on top of the world.

Relaxing Outdoors on a Sunny Day: When you are relaxing in your chair, reading your favourite book as the light breeze keeps the temperature under control, and the sun warms your skin, you feel at peace with the environment around you.

Making Someone smile: Sometimes you notice that your fellow student is under great stress due to the exams that are just coming up, so you invite them over to your place to just relax, have good food and watch a movie with a smile on their face as they enjoy yourself will make you the happiest.

Chapter 32:
Happy People Focus on What They Are Good at

Steve Jobs said, "Your work is going to fill a large part of your life, and the only way to be truly satisfied is to do what you believe is great work. And the only way to do great work is to love what you do." Your family and society put a lot of pressure on you for being a specific type of successful usually. That falls under the false lines of what society considers successful: being socially important and having a lot of wealth. Still, when you focus on money and superficial status, you will not be able to live a truly fulfilling life. Even when in your office you focus on tasks that you find difficult or displeasing, you will feel frustrated. Now, I quoted Steve Jobs in the start that man is a huge example for all of us; he focused on what he liked and eventually became successful.

You do not have to stray from your talents. If you enjoy doing something and it comes easily to you, there are high chances of being a leader in that field because you are naturally good at it. There is always the pressure of achieving what other people consider success, and you have to resist it. When you focus on things you are good at, you have to realize that when you focus on things you are good at, you do not have to try too hard things will eventually fall into place. That certainly does not mean that you never have to try new things. You should always take new opportunities because you can find things you are good at.

To know that you are good at something is another thing and to be modest about it is another. If you think someone would be interested in what you are good at, tell them. Let people know your skills because if there is a project or job prospect, people will know who they need to contact. Secondly, you can never be great at everything, so you should narrow your field of expertise and then practice those. That will help you grow. Plus, in your workplace, you do not need to shy away from new opportunities. If there are tasks, you think you are good at, volunteer for them. This way, your superiors will also get to know about your skills and interests, and you never know what they might have in store for you.

You need to be self-aware; if you think you are good at something, you probably because you will meet many people in life that will try to sidetrack you. They will tell you that people are not interested in what you are trying to sell or wasting your time and should do what everyone else is doing. Every person you meet will have an opinion of their own, but you need to remember you are the only one that has control over their life, so you do not need to be intimidated into thinking that what you are good at is not worth it.

Chapter 33: Why Spending Time with Friends Can Buy You Happiness

At times we quarrel with our friends, feel jealous of them, or even tattle about one another. So for what reason do we waste time with friends? Since they make us burst into laughter when we're sad. Since they're there to slap us on the back and raise a glass when we have uplifting news. What's more, since they play a featuring job in a portion of our most precious memories. You needn't bother with us to disclose to you that regardless of how confounded your platonic relationships may at times feel, your friendships improve your life in profoundly meaningful manners.

While the real advantages of friendships can't ever be measured (how do you calculate how a good deal pleasure your quality friend has added to you over the years?), look at it after looking at suggests that friendships raise our happiness or even our health. Here are some reasons why you need friends

Happiness Is Contagious

If a pal of ours is satisfied, we're much more likely to be, too. A Harvard Medical School takes a look at 5,000 humans over two decades. One person's happiness spreads via their social institution even up to a few tiers of separation and that the impact lasts so long as a year. On the turn side, unhappiness isn't as contagious: While having a pal who's satisfied improves your chance of being satisfied with the aid of using 15 percent, having one who's sad lowers your probabilities with the aid of using simply 7 percent. Fascinating!

The Happiest People are the Most Social

Convincing proof of this phenomenon comes from Ed Diener and Martin Seligman, the main specialists withinside the subject of happiness research. When they compared the happiest to the least satisfied human beings, they found that the primary institution became surprisingly social and had the most powerful courting ties. Exact social family members had been a need for human beings to sense satisfaction. Similarly, different psychologists have written that they want to belong as "fundamental."

Friends Cut the Small Talk—and That Makes Us Happy

Sure, all of us chit-chat with our buddies. However, while there's something critical to discuss, we have a confidant with a bit of luck with a bit of luck who we will flip to. That's essential because human beings with the very best stages of health have more "substantive" conversations than small talk, in keeping with 2010 have a look at in Psychological Science. When it turned into the final time, you had a significant communique with a pal? If you cannot remember, timetable a few catch-up times, stat!

Chapter 34:
How Will You Choose To Live Your Life?

How will you choose to live your life? This is something that only you have the power to decide.

We all want different things. As individuals, we are all unique and we have our own ideas about what it means to live a meaningful life. Some treasure family, friends, and relationships above all else, while others prioritise money, material things, careers, and productivity. There is no right or wrong to pursue or place any of these things on a pedestal. If your dream is to build a multi-billion dollar company, then go ahead and chase that dream. If you prioritise just being as stress-free as possible, to do as little work as you can, well you can choose to structure your life in such a way as well. As long as it works for you and that you are happy doing so, I would say go for it.

Sure, your priorities might change as you get older and wiser. Embrace that change. We are not always met to move in a linear fashion in life. We should learn to live like water, being fluid, ever-changing, ever-growing, ever-evolving. Our interests, priorities, passions, all change as we move from one stage of life to the next.

Some only realise that they might want to focus on relationships at a certain point in their lives, some might only want to start a family when they reach a certain age. The point is that we never truly know when is the time when we might feel ready to do something, as much as well tell ourselves that we will know.

The best thing we can do for ourselves right now, in this very moment, is to do what we think is best for us right now, and then to make tweaks and adjustments along the way as we travel down that road faithfully.

Trying to plan and control every aspects of our lives rarely ever works out how we imagined it. You see, life will give us lemons, but it can also give us durians. We might get thrown off the road through unexpected changes. Things that challenge our beliefs and our priorities. Health issues, family tragedies, financial meltdowns, natural disasters, these are things that we can never plan for. We may either choose to come out of these things with a clearer plan for our next phase of life, or we may choose to give up and not try anymore.

All of us have the power to choose how we want to live our lives in this very moment. The worst thing you can do right now is not know what your priorities are and to just cruise through life without having at least a short-term vision on what you want to get out of it.

Take the time to reflect every single day to work on that goal, however scary or simple it may be. Never take your eye off the post and just keep traveling down that path until you reach a fork in the road.

www.ingramcontent.com/pod-product-compliance
Lightning Source LLC
Chambersburg PA
CBHW070925080526
44589CB00013B/1429